Wager for More

A Christian Perspective on Online Sports and Casino Gambling

MAX ROGERS

ISBN 979-8-89243-933-6 (paperback)
ISBN 979-8-89243-934-3 (digital)

Christian Faith Publishing
832 Park Avenue
Meadville, PA 16335
www.christianfaithpublishing.com

Printed in the United States of America

INTRODUCTION

October 23, 2022
Yankee Stadium

After an 84-minute delay, game 4 of Major League Baseball's American League Championship Series is finally set to begin. The players in pinstripes take the field, led by star Aaron Judge as he confidently jogs to his position in right field. The Yankees' home crowd is restless. Their team is down three games to none against the Houston Astros. Another loss in this series would send them home for the season. Fortunately for the Yankees, their surprise star pitcher of the year, Nestor Cortez, is on the mound to start this make-or-break game. Nasty Nestor fires in a first-pitch fastball outside to leadoff hitter José Altuve. It is not until the third pitch, a cutter that Altuve takes for a strike, that the first applause from the home crowd emerges. Altuve works the count to 3–1 and then takes a slider from Cortez for strike two. The Yankees' crowd is on their feet, hoping for a punch-out to start the night. After Altuve fouls off another slider, he watches a cutter go just off the outside part of home plate. Altuve tosses his bat, thinking he has drawn a walk, but the home plate umpire calls strike three. The stadium explodes, and the Yankees fans waste no time hurling taunts at Altuve. In unison, the Bronx crowd chants obscenities as Altuve picks up his bat and walks back to the dugout.

Among the Yankees fans joining in the chants are four young men from Staten Island, seated in row 10 of section 135 in left field.

"Sit down, you cheater!"

Altuve's alleged involvement in the Astros' 2017 cheating scandal has not been forgotten by any baseball fan, especially those in New York. The Staten Island group is clad in Yankees gear and hasn't made the trip to the Bronx and endured a long rain delay to witness their team's season end.

Up next for the Astros is rookie shortstop Jeremy Peña. Just as Cortez delivers his first pitch to Peña, an unexpected shout comes from one of the Staten Island group members: "Come on, Peña! Just a base hit, Peña!"

Cortez's first-pitch cutter is fouled off by Peña, causing his three friends to turn and give their friend confused looks.

"What did you just say? Did you really just say, 'Come on, Peña'?"

The friend, sporting a Yankees hoodie and a backwards Yankees hat, innocently raises his hands in the air. "He's part of my parlay, guys. I just need Peña to get a hit!"

It all becomes clear to his friends and the rest of the section, me included, as we overhear their conversation. As the at-bat continues, our friend with the Yankees sweatshirt, momentarily rooting against his own team, gets his wish. On the eighth pitch of the at-bat, Peña smacks an eighty-four-miles-per-hour cutter from Cortez into left field.

"Yes, let's go!" shouts the young man who just secured one leg of his parlay. "All right, all right, we're good now. Let's go, Yanks!"

Overhearing such an odd interaction among what appeared to be die-hard Yankees fans isn't the craziest thing to witness in the fall of 2022. Online sports betting has taken the United States by storm over the last few years as more and more states made it legal.

As the third hitter for the Astros, Yordan Álvarez walks to the plate, I turn to my left to face my friend Pete. Earlier in the week, I invited Pete and his sixteen-year-old son James to the game. As both were Yankees fans, they made the drive from New Jersey to support their team. Curious about Pete's opinion on the current state of online sports betting, I ask him about it. Surely, he's somewhat aware, given the abundance of commercials for online betting during televised sports events.

Pete takes a deep breath and responds, "Well…my father-in-law got James a sports betting account, and he's been placing all kinds of bets with it. It's not his own money. His grandpa funds it. But he sure enjoys it."

James, a high school sophomore and a star midfielder on the soccer team, looks up from his phone and smiles.

Pete adds, with his typical humor, "He wanted to bet on the Yankees tonight, but I told him not to lose twice, so he bet on the Astros instead."

It turns out to be good advice from Pete. After falling behind 3–0 early, the Astros stage a remarkable comeback and clinch the game with a 6–5 victory, securing their spot in the World Series. As we all rise from our seats, accompanied by Frank Sinatra's iconic "New York, New York," I can't help but wonder how young James is feeling amid the Astros players' exuberant celebrations on the infield. Is he disappointed that his favorite team's season has come to an end? Or perhaps winning his bet is overshadowing any disappointment he might be feeling.

CHAPTER 1

How We Got Here

Gambling on sports in the United States is nothing new. Many baseball fans are familiar with the stories of Shoeless Joe Jackson and Pete Rose. However, the broad legalization of sports gambling in America is a recent phenomenon. Under the Professional and Amateur Sports Protection Act of 1992, it was illegal for states to authorize sports betting. There were only four states exempt from the 1992 ruling because of preexisting state laws that permitted some form of the activity. These states were Delaware, Montana, Nevada, and Oregon.

In 2018, the US Supreme Court struck down the 1992 act in *Murphy v. National Collegiate Athletic Association*. This ruling effectively allowed the other forty-six states to also legalize sports betting. If this law had been struck down in 1998 instead of 2018, the sports gambling industry would likely have followed the Las Vegas business model, establishing legal sports betting stations inside casinos, where prospective gamblers would be required to physically travel to a casino to place a bet. What was significant about 2018 was that it occurred during the "smartphone era" of American society. The ability to simply download an app to place any type of sports bet exponentially increased not only the potential gambling population but also the percentage of the population that is willing to participate.

There are currently thirty states in America (and Washington, DC) that allow some form of online gambling. Additionally, several other states are considering legislation to legalize online gambling. Unsurprisingly, the number of people seeking help for gambling issues has skyrocketed. The National Council on Problem Gambling stated that in 2021, calls to their helpline increased by 43 percent.

This impact is not limited to gamblers of legal age. According to the National Council on Problem Gambling, approximately 60% of high school–aged adolescents report having gambled for money during the past year, and male adolescents gamble more often than females.

While recent studies show the widespread addiction issues caused by the legalization of online sports and casino gambling in America, this book will not attempt to argue against the legality of gambling. This book, however, explores how faith in Jesus reorients one's view toward living for God's purposes in reaction to His love and sacrifice for us. When we do that, there is no longer a compelling purpose in gambling.

CHAPTER 2

A Common Story

To highlight a common story among young men in their teens and twenties, I downloaded one of the sports betting and casino apps on my phone in the summer of 2021. I placed a $5 wager on my favorite baseball team, the St. Louis Cardinals, to win their game that day. Fortunately, the Cardinals emerged victorious, and I was about $5 richer.

Several days passed, and I found myself growing somewhat bored with the $5 bets. First, the amount of money at stake did not seem substantial, and second, I had to wait for the lengthy three-hour baseball games to conclude before knowing the outcome. It was then that I noticed a Casino button at the top of the app and thought, *Why not give it a try? At least I'll find out if I win or lose immediately.* Intrigued by the prospect, I decided to play a game of blackjack, placing a $5 bet. To my delight, I emerged victorious, prompting me to place another $5 bet, which I won as well. By the end of the first day, I had accumulated approximately $50 and deemed it a reasonable stopping point. I acknowledged that I lacked the extraordinary skills of Dustin Hoffman's *Rain Man* character or a card counter. Nevertheless, over the following weeks, I continued to indulge in more and more blackjack games, with the self-imposed rule that if I ever lost the amount I had previously won, I would stop.

As I continued playing, I started betting more: $10 a hand, then $20 a hand. I was getting lucky, and eventually, I was up $500. My winning streak kept going, reaching $1,000, then $1,500. At this point, I was betting at least $100 per hand. Occasionally I would feel extra lucky and place even larger bets. I distinctly remember joining a live blackjack table just to experience it. I wagered $250 on the hand and was dealt a 10 and a 6, while the dealer had a 10 as an up card. If you know anything about blackjack, then you know that this is one of the worst hands you can be dealt. I was very likely to bust, but I stuck to my basic strategy card and hit my 16. It was a 5, making it 21—winner, winner, chicken dinner! The next day, I lost several bets worth several hundred dollars, but then I went on to bet $1,000—something that would have seemed unimaginable just a few days earlier. I won. Soon enough, I found myself up over $3,000, feeling like a magician.

My first lesson about how quickly things can go wrong when gambling online occurred when I switched to playing roulette. For the first spin, I picked black to win, but the virtual ball landed on a red number. I decided to play again, picking black again. Once more, it came up red. After fifteen spins of the wheel, there were thirteen reds and two green zeroes. I lost fifteen consecutive times until it finally landed on black. I immediately did the math on a calculator, and the odds of seeing the same color fifteen times in a row are about 1 in 49,423. So what had just happened was incredibly unlikely. So after losing $800 in ten minutes, I ended the roulette experiment and went back to blackjack. Like many blackjack players who stay at the table for too long, I gradually began losing my profits. As my balance dwindled, I attempted to recoup my losses through larger bets. This approach had worked for me before, but not this time. Before long, I lost the $3,000 of my previous winnings in addition to the $3000 I spent trying to recover my previous winnings.

I will never forget slouching down in the kitchen, wondering what in the world I had just done. I remember not being able to speak at dinner that night. At that moment, I experienced a profound sense of despair unlike anything I had ever felt before. I simply could not fathom how I had gone from making $5 bets to losing a staggering $6,000 in total. My mind was consumed by thoughts of what I could have done with that money. The most challenging aspect, however, was realizing that I still had the option to continue gambling to recoup my losses. Nevertheless, what I chose to do next was the best decision I could have made. I voluntarily placed myself on an exclusion list in New Jersey, effectively banning myself from online gambling for a minimum of five years. As much as I yearned to try to recover what I had lost, I recognized the danger of digging myself into an even deeper financial hole.

I told very few people what had happened. That is partly why I wrote this book: to highlight that the shame a person feels when losing money can make it incredibly difficult to admit what happened to the people who care about you the most. After a few days of attempting to refocus on work and struggling to take my mind off the money I had lost, I realized that one way to attempt to resolve the situation was by earning back the money.

I was fortunate to have the opportunity to compete in wrestling in both high school and college, and this experience eventually led me to coach younger athletes. After reaching out to the head coach of a local high school, I was given the opportunity to coach. Over the course of the season, coaching wrestling allowed me to recover money I had previously lost by gambling. Moreover, I formed meaningful connections with the coaches and athletes I worked with, and I am grateful that the negative experience ultimately transformed into a positive one, thanks to the guidance of the Lord. As I contemplated how I could assist others, I realized the importance of presenting an alternative perspective on gambling, given its prevalent advertising and online presence today. In my case, I turned to the Bible. After reading the New Testament, I discovered that while Jesus did not explicitly say, "Do not gamble," adhering to His teachings should keep us from ever considering gambling in the first place.

CHAPTER 3

WWJD?

Growing up in a Christian home and attending Sunday school, I am familiar with an acronym often taught to young people when they face a difficult decision, WWJD?, which stands for "What would Jesus do?" As we grow up, we encounter various forks in the road. For instance, when we are younger, we may wonder, *Should I lie to my parents about what time I came home from school?* or *Should I cheat on this science test? Susan is poorly hiding her answers in front of me.* As we transition into early adulthood, we face different questions, such as, "Should I watch porn? I am alone, and nobody will know" or "Should I get drunk with my friends tonight?" As independent adults, we may ask ourselves, "Should I go to church on Sunday?" If we consider what Jesus would do, most of these answers may seem straightforward in theory but can be challenging to put into practice. Personally, I can recall numerous occasions when I knew what Jesus would do, yet I chose to do the opposite anyway.

Let's start with the first story in the Bible when a human could have used the WWJD? acronym to make the right decision. After God created Adam, the Lord put him in the Garden of Eden to work in the garden and take care of it. God gave Adam one commandment to follow: "You are free to eat from any tree in the garden; but you must not eat from the tree of the knowledge of good and evil, for when you eat from it you will certainly die" (Genesis 2:16–17 NIV).

God then created a woman, Eve, to serve as a suitable helper and companion for Adam.

All was well in the garden until a crafty serpent said to Eve, "Did God really say, 'You must not eat from any tree in the garden'?" (Genesis 3:1 NIV). When Eve replied that they were not to eat from one specific tree in the middle of the garden, the serpent replied, "You will not certainly die… For God knows that when you eat from it your eyes will be opened, and you will be like God, knowing good and evil" (Genesis 3:4 NIV). The serpent tricked Eve with the notion that eating the fruit would provide all upside and no downside. The serpent would call it a "risk-free" bet. When Eve offered Adam the fruit from the forbidden tree, Adam chose to eat it. By listening to his wife rather than God, Adam made perhaps the greatest gamble in human history. As a result, sin entered the world and created a debt so large that only God Himself could bear it—through the death and resurrection of Jesus.

CHAPTER 4

Money and Greed

Why do people gamble? I gambled because I saw opportunities to make money quickly and easily with just a few clicks of a button. The definition of gambling according to Oxford Languages is "playing games of chance for money." Based on this simple definition, the core motivation behind gambling is the desire for financial gain.

Jesus frequently discusses money in His teachings. I believe He does so because He understands that for humans, it often occupies a prominent place in our thoughts. At a fundamental level, money offers the basic needs of food and shelter but also opportunities for security and leisure. Money is not evil, as great good can come from money to advance the kingdom of God. However, our attitude toward money is where the danger lies.

> Do not store up for yourselves treasures on earth, where moths and vermin destroy, and where thieves break in and steal. But store up for yourselves treasures in heaven, where moths and vermin do not destroy, and where thieves do not break in and steal. For where your treasure is, there your heart will be also. The eye is the lamp of the body. If your eyes are healthy, your whole body will be full of light. But if your eyes

are unhealthy, your whole body will be full of darkness. If then the light within you is darkness, how great is that darkness! No one can serve two masters. Either you will hate the one and love the other, or you will be devoted to the one and despise the other. You cannot serve both God and money. (Matthew 6:19–24 NIV)

Jesus discusses storing treasures not here on earth but in heaven. The question I believe Jesus wants us to ask ourselves is "What do I consider to be my treasure?" Is it money? Is it our wealth? Or is it something else? To Jesus, the treasure means believing in Him, following His teachings, giving to those in need, showing mercy to others, bringing peace to others, treating others as we would treat ourselves, and sharing God's love with others.

Should we take Jesus literally when He says, "Do not store up treasures on earth"? Is He suggesting that we should not save or possess any money for ourselves? I believe that Jesus uses hyperbole to convey His message. His intention, however, is clear: we should seek earthly treasures that are of the highest value in heaven. How can we achieve this? By keeping our focus, or "eyes," on what Jesus deems as true treasure and value. In summary, Jesus presents a stark contrast, highlighting the two sides in the battle of who we should serve: God or ourselves.

CHAPTER 5

Trusting in the Lord

If you are a Christian, can you recall the moment you placed your faith in Jesus? Some of you may have a specific moment when you accepted Jesus as your Lord and Savior. Others, like me, may have grown up in a Christian household, where going to church was always part of our lives. Jesus makes certain promises to those who choose to follow Him. However, with the busyness of our daily lives and the prevalence of sin in the world, it can be easy to forget His words and teachings in favor of pursuing the things the culture values.

While there is ongoing debate regarding whether gambling should be considered a sin, the teachings of Jesus oppose the practice of gambling. As Christians, we are taught that the money we earn through our work is honorable, but we also recognize that it is not solely ours. The wealth we accumulate is ultimately provided by God, as it belongs to Him. In the book of James, we read,

> Every good and perfect gift is from above, coming down from the Father of the heavenly lights, who does not change like shifting shadows. (James 1:17 NIV)

If God has bestowed a gift upon us, should we be willing to risk losing it through a game of chance? Are God's financial blessings not sufficient?

While Jesus does not specifically address the act of gambling and its implications for the money that He has provided us, He does emphasize throughout the New Testament that we, His followers, should trust Him to meet our needs. In His Sermon on the Mount, Jesus teaches that as Christians, we need not be consumed by worry.

> Therefore I tell you, do not be anxious about your life, what you will eat or what you will drink, nor about your body, what you will put on. Is not life more than food, and the body more than clothing? Look at the birds of the air: they neither sow nor reap nor gather into barns, and yet your heavenly Father feeds them. Are you not of more value than they? And which of you by being anxious can add a single hour to his span of life? And why are you anxious about clothing? Consider the lilies of the field, how they grow: they neither toil nor spin, yet I tell you, even Solomon in all his glory was not arrayed like one of these. (Matthew 6:25–34 NIV)

Then Jesus said to His disciples,

> Therefore I tell you, do not worry about your life, what you will eat; or about your body, what you will wear. For life is more than food, and the body more than clothes. Consider the ravens: They do not sow or reap, they have no storeroom or barn; yet God feeds them. And how much more valuable you are than birds! Who of you by worrying can add a single hour to your life? Since you cannot do this very little thing, why do you worry about the rest? (Luke 12:22–26 NIV)

There are many great pieces of wisdom we can take away from both Matthew's and Luke's recordings of Jesus's teachings. First, Jesus tells His disciples and followers not to be anxious about what to eat, drink, or wear. All these items pertain to the human body, and Jesus's point is that life in communion with Him is not about our bodies but rather about our spirits. Our physical bodies will eventually turn to dust, while our souls will be with Jesus in heaven. Obviously, Jesus does not expect us to take it literally by not eating, drinking, or wearing any clothes. Our focus should be on God's kingdom and not on earthly things. We should concentrate on living a life in accordance with how Jesus says we should live our life.

Why should we not worry about money? Because Jesus loves us more than birds! That may seem like a silly statement, but Jesus is quite clear in His message that animals like ravens don't work for money, and they would not be able to store it even if they could. God takes care of them, just as He takes care of us. Not only does Jesus say not to worry, but He also emphasizes that worrying is a waste of time!

CHAPTER 6

Being Aware of Those Who Are Untruthful

Do you like it when you are lied to? Probably not. There are two definitions of a lie. The first is "an intentionally false statement." The second definition is not as straightforward. It is used with reference to a situation involving deception or founded on a mistaken impression.

Over the last couple of years, it has been difficult to watch a sporting event on TV without seeing gambling advertisements. Almost every one of these advertisements offers something enticing for new customers, such as "no-sweat first bets" or "risk-free" bets. These companies want those who use their gambling sportsbooks or online casinos to believe that if they lose their first bet, the betting company will reimburse them for their losses. It may seem like a great deal, right? Is it too good to be true? Absolutely.

What they do not explain to you, the viewer, is that if you lose your bet, you do not get a simple refund for the amount that you lost. If I bet $100 on a sports or casino game and lose, I will not be credited with $100 that I can deposit back into my bank account and forget that this ever happened. These sportsbook sites instead give you back "free bets," and you need to re-bet those amounts to cash out any potential winnings. In this hypothetical scenario, the sportsbook company will give me $100 with which to gamble.

However, there is still a chance that this $100 in "free bets" will also be lost and that I will be left with nothing. This does not sound risk-free at all.

To provide further evidence of how these companies deceive potential customers, the NBA recently decided that sports betting operators can no longer use the term *risk-free* in their marketing language on platforms operated by the NBA and its franchises. According to a report from the *Sports Business Journal* (SBJ), Scott Kaufman-Ross, the NBA senior vice president in charge of gaming and new business ventures, stated, "It's important that we be clear with our fans that sports betting carries inherent risk. The notion that anything in this area is risk-free runs counter to the key messaging and education around sports betting. We just feel it's the right move for us." Sports betting partners will no longer be allowed to use the term *risk-free*.

While the NBA, like other major sports leagues, has embraced sports gambling, the people in charge of this league felt that they had to say something when it became evident that companies were using deceptive language to lure new customers into thinking they were taking no risks. Now, you may have noticed the term *no-sweat first bet* being used in place of *risk-free*. When someone says, "Hey, it's no sweat," it means that you should not worry about it; everything is fine. This is not true either. Losing a bet does not guarantee a refund. Instead, you merely receive additional resources through which you can increase your chances of developing a gambling addiction. These marketing tactics are neither honorable nor admirable.

When we consider lying in the Bible, many Christians will first refer to what the Ten Commandments say. Among the commandments inscribed on the tablets that Moses brought down from Mount Sinai to the Israelites, one specifically states,

> You shall not give false testimony against
> your neighbor. (Exodus 20:16 NIV)

In the New Testament, we find further support that God's will for us as humans is not to deceive one another. In Paul's letter to the Colossians, he writes,

> Do not lie to each other, since you have taken off your old self with its practices and have put on the new self, which is being renewed in knowledge in the image of its Creator. (Colossians 3:9–10 NIV)

Instead of lying to or deceiving others, what does the Lord wish for us to do instead? If we continue reading Paul's letter, we find the answer.

> Therefore as God's chosen people, holy and dearly loved, clothe yourselves with compassion, kindness, humility, gentleness, and patience. Bear with each other and forgive one another if any of you has a grievance against someone. Forgive as the Lord forgave you. And over all these virtues put on love, which binds them all together in perfect unity. (Colossians 3:12–14 NIV)

Paul's wisdom sums up Christian teaching succinctly, which is that we ought to love and forgive one another. While gambling companies encourage their users to engage in behaviors that have the potential to lead to financial ruin, it is important that, as Christians, we pray for them to change their ways.

CHAPTER 7

Not Modeling Detrimental Behavior

As Christians, the Bible's teachings not only apply to how our actions affect ourselves but also to how our actions impact others. This is especially true for those who are younger and may view older individuals as role models. Therefore, it becomes even more crucial for us to be conscious of our actions.

When others—friends and bystanders alike—see us gambling, it affirms to them that we believe our action has value. Since we have a limited amount of time each day, every activity we choose must be worthwhile, considering the countless alternatives available to us.

Jesus is quite clear that our behavior is of the utmost importance to others. In Mark's gospel, Jesus says,

> If anyone causes one of these little ones—
> those who believe in me—to stumble, it would
> be better for them if a large millstone were hung
> around their neck and they were thrown into the
> sea. (Mark 9:42 NIV)

The apostle Paul reinforces Jesus's message in his letter to the Romans.

> Therefore let us stop passing judgment on
> one another. Instead, make up your mind not

to put any stumbling block or obstacle in the way of a brother or sister. I am convinced, being fully persuaded in the Lord Jesus, that nothing is unclean in itself. But if anyone regards something as unclean, then for that person it is unclean. If your brother or sister is distressed because of what you eat, you are no longer acting in love. Do not by your eating destroy someone for whom Christ died. Therefore do not let what you know is good to be spoken as evil. For the kingdom of God is not a matter of eating and drinking, but of righteousness, peace and joy in the Holy Spirit, because anyone who serves Christ in this way is pleasing to God and receives human approval. Let us therefore make every effort to do what leads to peace and to mutual edification. Do not destroy the work of God for the sake of food. All food is clean, but it is wrong for a person to eat anything that causes someone else to stumble. It is better not to eat meat or drink wine or to do anything else that will cause your brother or sister to fall. So whatever you believe about these things keep between yourself and God. Blessed is the one who does not condemn himself by what he approves. But whoever has doubts is condemned if they eat, because their eating is not from faith; and everything that does not come from faith is sin. (Romans 14:13–23 NIV)

This passage from Paul provides an appropriate response to those who reason that gambling is acceptable because a majority of those who partake only do so in moderation as a form of entertainment. As much as gambling companies would like us to believe that their business model consists of moderate gamblers, studies show that they generate most of their profits from a small minority of heavy bettors. In New Jersey, a Rutgers University study by Lia Nower showed that approximately 5 percent of all sports bettors placed almost half of all bets and were responsible for nearly 70 percent of the total money gambled.

Paul encourages us never to put a stumbling block or hindrance in the way of a brother or sister. Sometimes, however, it is challenging for us to know what vices our family or friends are struggling with at any given time. Some people have difficulty with alcohol. Would it be wise to drink or encourage drinking around a person struggling with alcohol? Of course not. While it may be easy to spot someone with an alcohol problem, spotting someone who is struggling with gambling can be more difficult. Therefore, it is important for us as Christians to be conscious of our actions; this reinforces Jesus's will for us to engage in behavior that is healthy and encouraging.

CHAPTER 8

Earning Your Keep

If making a quick buck were easy, everyone would do it. Anyone who gambles does so not just to win money but also to earn it quickly with little effort. A game can last a couple of hours, an MMA fight could last a minute, and a blackjack hand could be won or lost in a few seconds. It is certainly possible to win cash quickly by gambling, but to do so, you must risk your capital. With that risk, if the result does not go your way, your capital will be lost to the casino or sportsbook.

While some may argue that a few dollars here and there do not matter much, the Bible encourages Christians to earn their living in a way that is pleasing to the Lord. In the creation story of Adam and Eve, which was referenced earlier, God placed them in the Garden of Eden to work. Humans have been working throughout the history of humankind. While not everyone enjoys getting up in the morning to go to their jobs, there are several reasons God encourages it.

For starters, working helps us provide for ourselves and our families, ensuring that we have enough to eat and have roofs over our heads. Working enables us to utilize the talents and gifts that God has bestowed upon us to glorify Him and support others. Our job is not only to work for God but also to work for the benefit of our neighbors. Regardless of the amount of money we earn from our jobs, we can also provide some financial support to individuals in need and worthy organizations.

Paul writes in his letter to the Colossians that if we focus on working for the Lord, He will provide for all our needs.

> Whatever you do, work at it with all your heart, as working for the Lord, not for human masters, since you know that you will receive an inheritance from the Lord as a reward. It is the Lord Christ you are serving. (Colossians 3:23–24 NIV)

When we gamble what we have earned through our labor, we risk things beyond the money itself. We are not acting as good stewards with the resources that God has provided for us. He gave us the ability to work so that we may provide for ourselves, our families, and others. The $100 lost by betting on an NFL game could have been used for the benefit of a struggling family member or a needy organization. Gambling does not demonstrate strength of character. At best, it can be a source of entertainment that could serve better purposes—for example, helping family, friends, a church, charities, etc. At its worst, gambling can lead to lost savings, lost jobs, broken families, poor health, or depression and leave us unable to assist those whom God has tasked us to serve.

CHAPTER 9

Giving

Jesus speaks about giving in many of his teachings. One particularly powerful story is found in the Gospel according to Luke.

> As Jesus looked up, he saw the rich putting their gifts into the temple treasury. He also saw a poor widow put in two very small copper coins. "Truly I tell you," he said, "this poor widow has put in more than all the others. All these people gave their gifts out of their wealth, but she, out of her poverty, put in all she had to live on." (Luke 21:1–4 NIV)

In Paul's second letter to the Corinthians, he writes,

> Remember this: Whoever sows sparingly will also reap sparingly, and whoever sows generously will also reap generously. Each of you should give what you have decided in your heart to give, not reluctantly or under compulsion, for God loves a cheerful giver. And God is able to bless you abundantly, so that in all things at all times, having all that you need, you will abound in every good work. (2 Corinthians 9:6–8 NIV)

The moment we gamble, our hearts turn away from a giving mentality. Instead, our focus becomes "What can I win?" or "How can I enrich myself?" Even if it is a small bet, as low as $5, it distracts us from serving God. Jesus wants to be involved in every aspect of our lives, including the healthy habits of spending time with friends and loved ones. There's nothing wrong with watching a sporting event, but incorporating gambling into our social time tugs at the strings of greed and distracts us from being engaged with our family, friends, and neighbors.

To better understand the differences between having a giving versus a greedy nature, consider the emotions you experience when you see a charity commercial on television. For instance, Shriners Hospital aims to raise funds for children with disabilities, and its commercials feature children sharing their stories and appealing for assistance to sustain the hospital's valuable operations. Another example is the Tunnels to Towers organization, which supports veterans who have lost limbs while serving for the United States. I have personally watched these commercials and felt impressed by the impactful work they do, which led me to donate.

On the flip side, what emotions do we feel when we see a sports betting or online casino commercial? These commercials aim to make every viewer who is watching them, whether they have gambled before or not, dream about winning money. The focus shifts inward toward how we can further enrich ourselves, which is the opposite of thinking about helping others.

CHAPTER 10

Being Made Whole

In my experience with gambling, everything was "hunky-dory" when I was winning money. Once I started losing, I did what is commonly referred to as chasing losses, or continuing to gamble to win back that money. This is a common problem while gambling. Initially, there were periods when I lost a bit but would soon gain it back again. However, things took a turn when I started repeatedly losing, and I began increasing my bets to recoup everything. The power of exponents got the best of me.

Being down money in betting is quite similar to experiencing a loss of something that's important to you. For me, it's like the feeling I had when I lost wrestling matches in high school or college. However, there is one glaring difference. I can't go back and change the outcomes of those athletic competitions. But with gambling, I can pull out a betting app or drive to a casino and try to break even.

While the negative feelings associated with losing a significant amount of money may never completely fade away, I can deal with them by turning to the teachings of the Bible on finding purpose and fulfillment. Fortunately, here on earth, Jesus is the ultimate source of forgiveness, regardless of the circumstances.

Jesus declared,

> I praise you, Father, Lord of heaven and
> earth, because you have hidden these things from

the wise and learned, and revealed them to little children. Yes, Father, for this is what you were pleased to do. All things have been committed to me by my Father. No one knows the Son except the Father, and no one knows the Father except the Son and those to whom the Son chooses to reveal him. Come to me, all you who are weary and burdened, and I will give you rest. Take my yoke upon you and learn from me, for I am gentle and humble in heart, and you will find rest for your souls. For my yoke is easy and my burden is light. (Matthew 11:25–30 NIV)

Jesus promises us eternal peace when we put our faith in Him. He sacrificed His life on the cross so that we may be made whole in heaven. There is no problem too great that would stop Jesus from lifting our chins up and telling us that it is okay, that we are forgiven, that we can go on living our lives in peace, and that we can change behaviors by changing our focus and the way we think. Gambling takes our focus away from the Lord, but if we place Jesus first, there is nothing that we cannot do or receive consistently with God's plan.

CHAPTER 11

Gratitude for God's Kingdom

In closing, I would like to leave you with a few words on how we can advance God's kingdom here on earth. Whether it is gambling, a different addiction, or a strained relationship, there are numerous struggles that Christians may be going through. During these struggles, it may seem like we are losing control; however, God is always in control, and He will direct our path if we put our faith in Him and seek to live for His purposes. In the moments of questioning, we need to decide if we want to live for God's kingdom or for our own kingdom. Do we trust God to provide for our needs, or do we think we have it all figured out?

If we would like to advance God's kingdom and place our faith in Him, we first need to be thankful for everything God has provided us in this life. Whether that be family, friends, shelter, or food, our basic needs and more have been fully met. As we approach God with our requests on changing our behaviors and ways to better serve Him, being grateful is the first step in pursuing God's kingdom to experience the perfect joy He intended for us.

In his letter to the church of Philippi, Paul reiterates that being grateful is the key to living a life that prioritizes the kingdom of God.

> Do not be anxious about anything, but
> in every situation, by prayer and petition, with
> thanksgiving, present your requests to God. And

the peace of God, which transcends all under-
standing, will guard your hearts and your minds
in Christ Jesus. (Philippians 4:6–7 NIV)

By approaching God with a grateful heart, God will provide us with the only peace that can fill all earthly voids. The temptations of this world seek to separate us from that peace. While I am still prone to make mistakes, I no longer gamble because I am reminded daily through the Word of God that I am blessed by Him and that no amount of money won on games of chance will increase or change the love God has for me. Choosing to live for God may seem hard, but struggling with sin is harder. We as Christians can bravely choose to follow God with gratitude.

ABOUT THE AUTHOR

Max Rogers is a follower of Jesus Christ, a husband, a brother, and a son. He was raised in New Jersey and has a degree in economics from Princeton University. Max enjoys volunteering as a youth wrestling coach in his spare time and is an avid fan of the St. Louis Cardinals. Max works in real estate asset management for a church endowment in New York City, where he resides with his wife, Tara.